Eye on Ancient Egypt

by L. L. Owens

Perfection Learning® CA

About the Author

Lisa L. Owens grew up in the Midwest. She has been writing since she was a little girl. And she has always loved to learn about people from different cultures.

She studied English and journalism at the University of Iowa. She has worked as a reporter, a proofreader, and an editor. Her interests include music and literature.

Ms. Owens now lives near Seattle with her husband, Timothy Johnson. He is an engineer. The two of them love watching old movies, trying new cooking styles, and exploring the beautiful Pacific Northwest.

Image credits: Art Today pp. 3, 5, 6, 8, 11 (top), 12, 13 (top, middle), 14, 15, 17, 18 (top, middle), 19 (top, middle), 20 (top), 21 (bottom), 22, 23 (bottom), 25, 27, 29, 31, 32, 33, 34, 35, 36, 37, 39, 40, 41, 42, 43, 44, 45, 46, 47, 49, 50, 51 (top, second, third), 53, 54; Corel cover (back), pp. 7, 11 (bottom), 13 (bottom), 16, 18 (bottom), 19 (bottom), 20 (bottom), 21 (top), 23 (top), 24, 26, 30, 38, 48 (bottom), 51 (bottom), 52, CyberPhoto cover (front), pp. 28, 48 (top); Library of Congress p. 10.

For information, contact
Perfection Learning® Corporation,
1000 North Second Avenue,
P.O. Box 500, Logan, Iowa 51546-1099.
Phone: 1-800-831-4190 • Fax: 1-712-644-2831
Paperback 0-7891-2855-1
Cover Craft® 0-7807-7836-7

Table of Contents

Introduction

Step into Ancient Egypt

Egypt has a long and great history. You've probably heard stories about the **pyramids,** the Great Sphinx, King Tut, or Cleopatra. And you probably know that they all existed in ancient Egypt.

Ancient means "very old." And Egypt is one of the oldest societies, or **cultures.** In fact, proof of Egyptian farming goes back to 4000 B.C.!

It's hard for people to know true dates when some things happened. Especially when they're looking at ancient times. So all the dates in the book are close guesses.

This book will give you a look at ancient Egypt. You'll see how people lived. What they believed. And you'll get a peek at some of Egypt's most interesting rulers.

Before you read on, look at the timeline. Where do you fit in? What about other events in history?

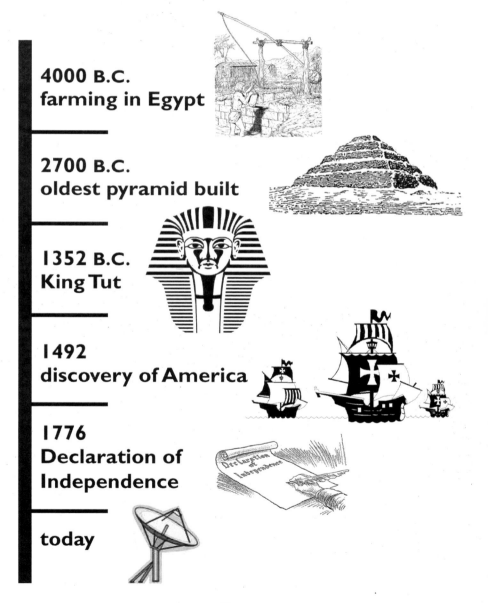

4000 B.C.
farming in Egypt

2700 B.C.
oldest pyramid built

1352 B.C.
King Tut

1492
discovery of America

1776
Declaration of Independence

today

Chapter 1

The World Is Born

*An Egyptian **legend** tells
how the world was created.*

Once upon a time, there was only darkness.

Then came a god named Nun. He was the big, black sea.

Nun reached out in all directions. Farther than any eye could see. Or any mind could understand.

Nun was in **chaos.** He had no shape. But he held hope for all things.

 There was another god. His name was Ra. He was the sun god. And he would bring order to the chaos of Nun.

One day, Ra rose from the water. He shot across the sky. He left stars along the way. Then he dove back into the ocean.

At last, he came out again. Now he was the sunrise. He lit the earth. And he made life possible.

Nun still lived. He lived beyond the world. He lived within the waters of the earth.

Ancient Egyptians tried to follow Ra's path. They tried to bring order to chaos. They tried to make life on the earth and in the **afterlife** easier and more fun.

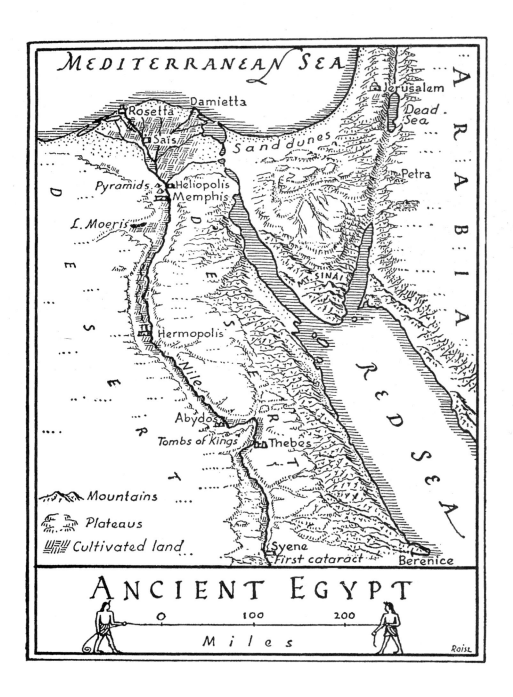

ANCIENT EGYPT

0   100   200
Miles

Chapter 2

Life on the Nile

Egypt is known as "the gift of the Nile."

To the people, the Nile river was very important. It watered their crops. It gave them fish to eat. And they could travel by boat on it.

So people built villages along its banks.

The Nile is a river. It is 1,200 miles long. And in some places, it is 12 miles wide. It flows south to north. That's why Upper Egypt was in the south. And Lower Egypt was in the north.

Working the Land

Huge **deserts** are on both sides of the river. It is very hot and very dry in Egypt. So it was hard to grow food.

The river flooded once a year. The land was soaked. Now farmers could grow their crops. This made them happy.

Most people were farmers. They grew apples, grapes, dates, and figs. They also

grew olives, carrots, wheat, barley, and flax to make **linen** for clothes.

Farmers also raised animals, such as cattle, antelope, goats, pigs, sheep, ducks and geese.

By 3200 B.C., Egyptians were ruled by one king. He was called a *pharaoh.*

The pharaoh owned all the land. So farmers had to pay a tax to him. This happened each year after harvest.

Other Trades

Farming was common. But there were many other jobs in Egypt. Here are just a few.

A smith made rings, necklaces, vases, and other items out of metal.

A painter decorated stone walls or wooden furniture.

A mason built things with bricks or stone.

A leather tanner prepared animal skins. They were used to make straps, bags, and sandals.

A carpenter built furniture and boats.

A baker made breads and cakes.

Egyptian women held many jobs too. Some were jobs that only men held in other societies.

Some women brewed beer. Some steered ships. Others gave advice to kings and queens.

Home Life

Houses were made of mud. Windows were small. This helped keep out the hot sun.

There was usually a kitchen, a living room, a bedroom, and a hall.

The flat roof was used as an extra room.

Workers and their families ate lots of bread, cheese, beans, and salad. They drank water.

Wealthy people ate the best baked goods. They ate meat too. They enjoyed beef, pork, and hyena. Goose and fish were also eaten. These people drank beer and wine.

People ate with their fingers. They only had knives to use.

Adults ate at a simple table. They sat on stools. But the children sat on the floor.

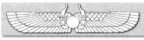

Egyptian men wore **kilts.** Women wore ankle-length dresses. It was very hot. So very young children rarely wore clothes at all.

Chapter

Life Goes On

Egyptians believed in life after death. They thought life went on in another world.

Life in the other world would be like life on Earth. However, in the other world, everything was beautiful and people were always happy.

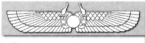

Farmers planned to keep working after death. They would farm the fields in the afterlife. These fields were thought to be perfect in every way.

A pharaoh was also expected to live on. He would spend the next life in a new kingdom.

The kingdom would be ruled by the god of the dead.

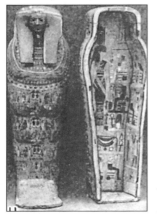

Of course, a pharaoh would need to take his things with him. He'd want to be comfortable.

So a pharaoh's tomb was filled with riches. He'd take gold, jewelry, and pottery. He took figures of gods. He even took food and drink!

Stories were written on the walls. Writers used *hieroglyphics*, or **symbols.** A symbol could stand for a sound or an idea.

These symbols look simple. But they can say as much as modern language.

Artists also spent years painting pictures on the walls. They painted scenes from the king's old life. They painted scenes from his next life.

They always showed the king as happy and rich in the next life. They thought the pictures would make it come true.

A royal tomb was often sealed in an underground burial room.

This room was deep inside a pyramid. Read on to learn more about these huge buildings.

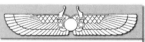

Queen Nefertari had a favorite game. She made sure it was in her tomb. The game was senet. The name means "passing."

An artist painted a scene with her winning the game. It was thought that winning would help her pass safely into the afterlife.

Chapter 4

The Pyramids

The Egyptians didn't multiply or divide. But they understood **geometry.** They had to in order to build the pyramids.

Most pyramids were the final resting places of pharaohs and their queens.

Why did the Egyptians choose the pyramid shape?

For one thing, it was hard for thieves to get into a pyramid. It was even harder to find the burial room.

But Egyptian legend says more about the shape.

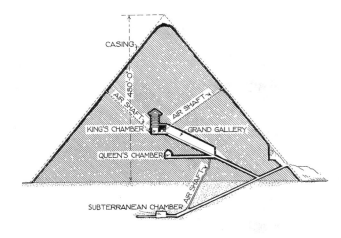

CASING

AIR SHAFT

480' 0"

AIR SHAFT

KING'S CHAMBER

GRAND GALLERY

QUEEN'S CHAMBER

AIR SHAFT

SUBTERRANEAN CHAMBER

The pyramid was like a giant hill. The same hill that Ra climbed when he left the waters of Nun.

It also stood for the rays of sunshine that fell upon Earth. The sun was thought to give life to the king inside.

The first pyramid was built for Pharaoh Zoser. It was at Sakkara. And it was built around 2700 B.C.

There were about 30 pyramids in ancient Egypt. But over many years, all have lost their riches to robbers.

The Great Pyramid at Giza was built around 2500 B.C. It was for Pharaoh Khufu. It still stands. Two others stand nearby.

The Great Pyramid probably took over 20 years to build.

It stands 480 feet high. The base is about 760 feet long. And it covers about 13 acres of land.

It was built from 2.6 million stone blocks. Some blocks weighed as much as 15 tons!

Try To Imagine

How much time is 20 years?

Five U.S. presidents could serve during that time. And a child could grow up and finish college.

How tall is 480 feet?

It's about as tall as 80 six-foot-tall men.

How long is 760 feet?

It's about as long as 2½ American football fields.

How much land is 13 acres?

It's about as much land as would be used to build 75 houses in a city.

How many items are in 2.6 million?

It's about how many people lived in Chicago, Illinois, in 1996.

How heavy is 15 tons?

It's about as heavy as 8 cars.

Work gangs placed one block at a time on a sled. Then they dragged it up ramps. Finally, the workers pushed the block into place.

Workers followed the sled. They helped push the sled around corners.

Accidents were common. Sometimes, a block would fall off the sled. The workers would be unable to stop it.

They might get crushed. Or they might fall to the ground. Many workers' lives were lost each year.

Modern builders tried to build a pyramid. They used the old ways. They wanted to understand what the ancient Egyptians went through.

They were able to make a small one. It was about 15 feet high. But they didn't think they could build one as big as those at Giza.

Chapter

I Want My Mummy!

Rulers spent their lives preparing for death. First they built a pyramid. They ordered special artwork. And they collected riches.

When a king or queen died, there was still much work to do.

It took over two months to prepare a body for burial. After all, the body had to be **preserved.** It had to last forever.

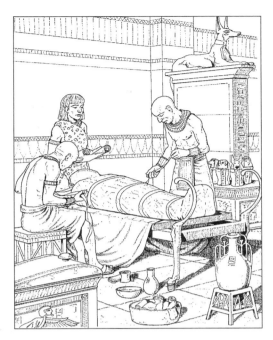

Priests did this work. They washed and dried the body. Then they removed all the organs, except the heart. And they stuffed the body with linen.

Next, they wrapped the body. They used layers of bandages and linen sheets. Gems and religious objects were placed between layers.

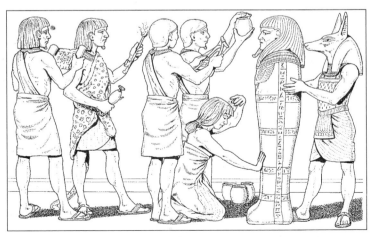

Finally, a decorated mask was placed on the head. And the **mummy** was ready.

It was placed in a wooden or plaster coffin. And the coffin was sealed in the tomb.

Sometimes, a mummy was placed in the smallest of three coffins. The coffins were then placed one inside the other.

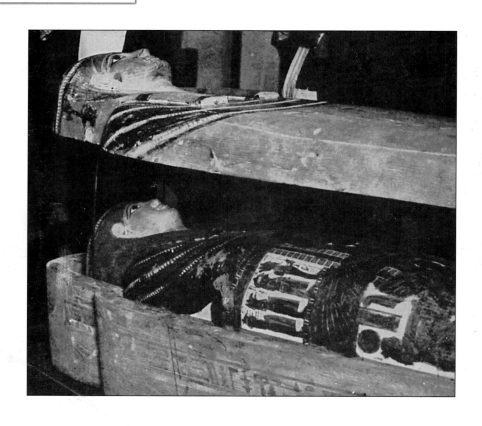

Chapter 6

King Tut

Tutankhamen married a king's daughter at age 10.

When the king died, Tut rose to the throne. He was 12.

Much of King Tut's **reign** remains a mystery. But he died in about 1352 B.C. And he was buried at Thebes in the Valley of the Kings.

Most of the tombs were robbed. Fortunately, King Tut's was not.

Howard Carter was an **archaeologist.** He found Tut's tomb in 1922.

He opened the door to the burial room. He held up a candle. And he peered inside.

He was thrilled. Nothing seemed to have been moved. And it had been over 3,000 years!

A member of his group was nervous. "Can you see anything?" he asked.

"Yes!" Dr. Carter replied. "Wonderful things!"

He saw strange animals, statues, and gold.

"Everywhere, the gleam of gold," he said.

Other objects were made of bronze, glass, silver, and ivory.

The room was filled with all kinds of riches. Everything Tut might need in his next life was there.

Dr. Carter studied the pictures inside. Some were drawn on the walls. Some were painted on furniture. Others were **etched** in gold vases. All showed scenes from Tut's daily life.

It was clear that Tut had loved to hunt. It was clear that he had a good sense of humor and that he loved his wife.

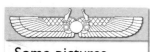

Some pictures were carved into the tomb's stone walls. Others were painted. The artists used water-based paints. They sometimes added honey, tree gum, or egg white to the paint. This made the color richer.

A scene on Tut's throne showed the young queen. She was dabbing perfume on Tut's collar.

Another picture showed Tut hunting with his lion cub.

There was a funny scene too. It showed the king and queen together. The queen was handing Tut an arrow. And she was pointing at a big, fat duck.

It is thought that King Tut ruled for only

eight years. He didn't have time to become important to his people.

But his tomb has really helped modern **scholars.** It's a big reason why we know so much about ancient Egypt.

Now Tut is one of the best-known
pharaohs in history. And all because his
tomb was never robbed.

Chapter 7

Queen Cleopatra VII

Cleopatra ruled from 51 B.C. to 30 B.C. She was a small woman with golden skin. Her hair was auburn. And her eyes were gray. They were said to turn violet when she was angry.

Cleopatra enjoyed her life. She was spirited and very smart. She liked the arts and sciences. And she was very interested in *astronomy*. That's the study of the stars.

Little is known about Cleopatra's life. But the story of her death is well-known.

In 30 B.C., Octavian had taken over Egypt. He was from Rome.

Cleopatra's husband, Mark Antony, was dead. And Cleopatra was a prisoner.

She was held in the vault that contained her tomb. It was a huge marble building.

She had already moved many of her things there. She had gold, jewels, ebony, ivory, **incense,** and spices.

**L a n g u a g e s
Cleopatra Spoke**

Egyptian
Greek
Latin
Ethiopian
Hebrew
Arabic
Syrian
Persian

She knew that Octavian would take her to Rome. He planned to kill her in front of his people. But she didn't want her life to end that way.

So Cleopatra prepared to kill herself.

She ate supper. She took a bath. She put on a white silk dress and her royal crown. Then she fastened an **amethyst** at her waist.

Meanwhile, her trusted maids scattered rose petals. They burned incense. And lit shaded lamps.

Cleopatra sat on her dining couch. She wrote a letter to Octavian.

Then, she called to one of the guards. She asked him to deliver the letter. It contained her will and a request to be buried with Mark Antony.

Another guard delivered a basket to her. He said it had figs in it. The figs were covered with green leaves.

"They're from an old man," said the guard. "He said the leaves protect the fruit from the sun."

But Cleopatra knew what was really under the leaves. The basket had come from Olympus. He was her doctor and trusted friend.

"I wish to be alone with my maids," said Cleopatra. "If you please."

The guard returned to his post.

Cleopatra sat on her golden bed. Her

maids fussed over her. They piled pillows around her.

Finally, she was ready. She reached into the basket. And she lifted out an **asp.**

Olympus had told her that the asp was poisonous. Its bite would cause a quick, painless death.

Cleopatra sighed. And she raised the asp to her neck.

Octavian found her a short time later. She looked peaceful. At first, he thought she was sleeping.

But the queen was dead!

Think About It
Cleopatra was born in 69 B.C. She was closer in time to us than she was to the pyramid builders.

Chapter 8

What Was Happening?

Do you wonder what else went on in ancient Egypt? Here's a brief look.

Geography

3400 B.C. to 3200 B.C. • There were two kingdoms in the Nile Valley. They were Upper Egypt and Lower Egypt.

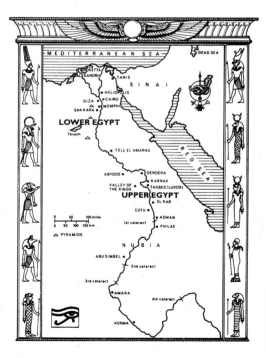

3200 B.C. to 3000 B.C. • Upper and Lower Egypt became one country—Egypt.

44

Arts & Crafts

3800 B.C. to 3600 B.C. ● People made polished bowls. Clay figures. Ivory combs. And **cosmetics.**

3400 B.C. to 3200 B.C. ● Jars were made out of stone blocks.

3200 B.C. to 3000 B.C. ● Harps, drums, and reed pipes were played.

2500 B.C. ● Jewelry was made from glass and glazed beads.

1600 B.C. to 1520 B.C. ● Egyptian love songs were sung at feasts.

Glass bottles appeared in 1500 B.C.

Math & Science

2700 B.C. • The first 365-day calendar was invented by the Egyptians.

1840 B.C. to 1760 B.C. • The Egyptian *cubit* was a unit of measurement. It was the length from the elbow to the fingertip.

1400 B.C. • The Egyptian water clock kept time. Water drained from small buckets. The water level marked the hours.

Farming & Business

3200 B.C. to 3000 B.C. • Boats had square sails and many oars. Reed boats sailed on the Nile.

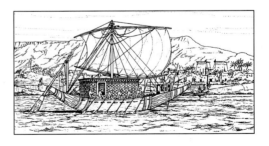

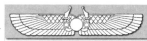

Farmers' plows took the form of a forked branch.

𓀀 𓂧 𓅐

3000 B.C. to 2800 B.C. • Canals were built.

Improved farming methods caused **population** growth.

𓀀 𓂧 𓅐

2500 B.C. • Wooden boats appeared.

𓀀 𓂧 𓅐

1840 B.C. to 1760 B.C. • Perfume was made from fruit oils.

𓀀 𓂧 𓅐

1360 B.C. to 1280 B.C. • Coins were made from copper.

Here's what Egyptian doctors were suggesting in 1200 B.C.

To cure an earache
1. Make an ointment out of sweet clover.
2. Put it in the ears.

To treat an open wound to the head
1. Sew up the wound.
2. Place fresh meat on it for the first day. Don't bandage.
3. Place the patient on his usual diet. Or tie him to a post. (Just until the wound begins to heal.)
4. Then treat the wound with fat, honey, and bandages every day.

To cure a headache
1. Grind reeds, juniper, tree gum, pitch, and berries.
2. Place mixture on head.
3. Wait for the pain to go away.

Chapter 9

What Did It Mean?

A *symbol* is something that stands for something else.

The dove is a worldwide symbol for peace. In America, the U.S. flag is a symbol of freedom.

The ancient Egyptians used symbols everywhere. They turned up on everyday objects and works of art. And they were carefully placed in pharaohs' tombs.

Take a look at these common Egyptian symbols. Have you seen them anywhere?

Ankh • Stood for everlasting life.

Crook • Meant "to rule" in hieroglyphics.

Eye of Horus, Lord of the Skies • The eye saw everything.

Ibis • Symbol of wisdom. Often buried with the dead.

Jackal • The guardian of the dead.

Scarab Beetle • Symbol of rebirth.

Sphinx • Sphinx at Giza

Symbol of all wisdom. It existed in Egyptian myth long before the Great Sphinx was built.

The basic sphinx had a female human head and the body of a bull. It had the feet of a lion and the wings of an eagle.

The Great Sphinx was built around 2500 B.C. It is at Giza near the pyramids.

It has the head of a woman and the body of a lion. And it was thought to hold the answer to the riddle of human life.

A Dream World

The Egyptians also had a great
interest in the symbols of their dreams.

They believed that they "awoke" in
their dreams. But they were in a different
world. And that was how they could
predict the future.

This is what they thought some of their dreams meant.

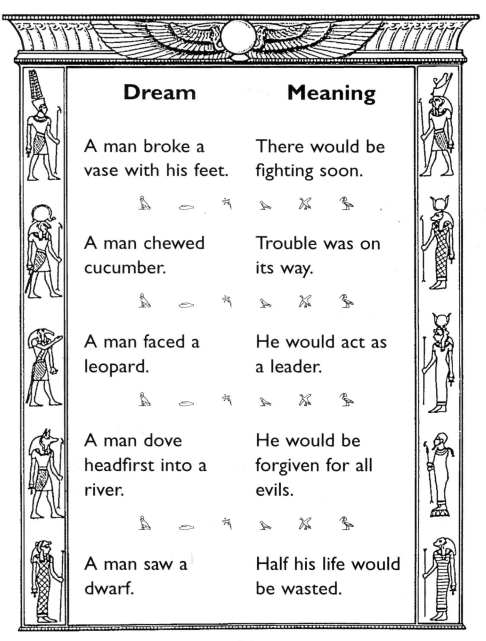

Dream	Meaning
A man broke a vase with his feet.	There would be fighting soon.
A man chewed cucumber.	Trouble was on its way.
A man faced a leopard.	He would act as a leader.
A man dove headfirst into a river.	He would be forgiven for all evils.
A man saw a dwarf.	Half his life would be wasted.

Conclusion

Back to the Future

Are you surprised at life in ancient Egypt? It was a long time ago. But the people were a lot like you.

The Egyptians worked hard. They enjoyed the arts. They battled nature. They fought wars. And they tried every day to improve their lives.

Modern people will continue to study the Egyptian culture. There are still many unanswered questions.

Do you have any?

GLOSSARY

afterlife   life after death in another world

amethyst   a light-purple gem

asp   a small snake. It is sometimes called an Egyptian cobra.

archaeologist   one who studies past civilizations

chaos   confusion

cosmetics   makeup

culture   a society. Also, the beliefs and habits of a group of people. The people usually live in the same region.

desert   hot, dry region with few plants or animals

etch   to create a design in metal or wood

geometry   the use of math to study shapes

incense	a fragrant material. Burning it releases its scent.
kilt	a knee-length skirt
legend	a story that's passed down over many years
linen	a type of cloth
mummy	a body that has been protected before burial
population	the number of people in an area
preserve	to protect from rotting; also, to save
pyramid	an ancient Egyptian structure. It has a square base. The walls are four triangles that meet at the top.
reign	the length of time a king or queen rules
scholar	one who seeks knowledge
symbol	something that stands for something else